WORLD VIEW
P U B L I S H I N G
R E N O • N E V A D A

PRINTED IN THE UNITED STATES OF AMERICA

Written & Compiled by:
Jeffrey Lawrence Benjamin
John Oliver
Michael Kitson
Lloyd Barnes
Todd C. Rich

Book design by Mike Kitson
Cover Design by On-Call Graphics, Inc.

World View Publishing
COPYRIGHT © 1999, World View Publishing
All rights reserved
First Published in 1997
Printed in the United States of America
99 98 97 96 95 12 11 10 9 8 7 6

Library of Congress Catalog Card Number: 97-72292

ISBN 0-9646800-1-7

II

WORLD VIEW
PUBLISHING
RENO • NEVADA

Also by these authors:
Quotes to Remember - A Guide to Wisdom
How to Get What You Want Now! - Real Life Habits for Success
101 Stress Busting Strategies - Real Life Habits for Success

iii

Special Thanks:
Kimberly Mills
Darrell Brown
Amy Prochaska
John Eliason

Aknowledgments:
David Driscoll & John Gilbert

Dedicated to the like-minded

FOREWORD

You hold in your hands a collection of proven habits! Habits that will help you transform your life through the power of effective communication.

Why is communication so important? Communication is vital for creating and maintaining effective relationships with family and friends. In the business world, your job requires you to get along with others so you can exchange ideas with co-workers and customers to achieve goals. And how well you communicate with yourself ultimately determines who you are and what you can achieve.

v

This book has been created to assist you in identifying the relevant, yet sometimes subtle or overlooked ways in which you can communicate more effectively. If you want to enhance your relationships, increase your self-awareness or achieve more in your professional endeavors, you must improve the way in you communicate.

We are confident these habits, when practiced, will have a significant impact in all areas of your life!

1. A positive attitude is contagious, so create an epidemic!

2. Listen to your inner voice.

"To master your mind,
you must first master
your thoughts."

~ The Mastermind

3.   Allow your communication to reveal your integrity.

4.   Promise service and terms you know you can deliver.

"You cannot perform in a manner inconsistent with the way you see yourself."

~ Dr. Joyce Brothers

5.   Avoid defining or judging others.

6.   Find similarities with others to create common ground.

"I don't like that man. I must get to know him better."

~ Benjamin Franklin

7.   Do not let who you were yesterday determine who you will be tomorrow.

8.   Give yourself a positive message every morning, first thing in the morning.

8

"If your happiness depends on what someone else says, I guess you do have a problem."

~ Richard Bach

9.   Be open to new thoughts because
     great communicators take in
     everything.

10. If you don't know the meaning of a
     word—look it up.

"Nothing pains some people
more than having to think."

~ Martin Luther King, Jr.

11. Encourage children to dream.

12. Treat and respect children as individuals rather than as objects.

"What you say to children sets the foundation for the rest of their lives."

~ The Mastermind

13. Follow the ratio of listening two-thirds of the time to talking one-third of the time.

14. Avoid overreacting. Get all the facts before beginning any new discussions.

"The only way to get the best of an argument is to avoid it."

~ Dale Carnegie

15. Demonstrate integrity by being honest with yourself and others.

16. When you communicate that you're going to do something, follow through.

"When in doubt tell the truth."

~ Mark Twain

17. Communication is a two-way street; know when to yield.

18. You can talk yourself into or out of anything.

"No one can hurt you without your consent."

~ Eleanor Roosevelt

19. Questioning is an art, so become an artist.

20. Remember: a question not asked is an answer not given.

"Judge a man not by his
answers, but by his questions."

~ Voltaire

21.   If ever in doubt, always ask
      someone to explain.

22.   Always make yourself clear by
      repeating your message.

"Perception appears to be automatic, but in fact it is a learned phenomenon."

~ Deepak Chopra

23. Before presenting an opinion, get the facts, think, then act.

24. Be careful when correcting others; you might offend them.

"Use soft words and hard arguments."

~ English Proverb

25. When receiving instructions paraphrase and explain what you heard.

26. If there is any possibility of not remembering something, write it down with the date and time.

"I asked my caddie for a sand wedge; ten minutes later he came back with a ham on rye."

~ Chi Chi Rodriguez

27. Ardently visualize the outcome of your goals.

28. Avoid comparing yourself to anyone except the you that you can be.

"We lift ourselves by our thought; we climb upon our vision of ourselves."

~ Orison Swett Marden

29. Increase your value by doing for customers things you don't necessarily get paid for.

30. Encourage feedback. It clarifies what you are conveying to others.

"It is a commitment to excellence, not title, that makes you a success."

~ The Mastermind

31. Always pay promptly, as it demonstrates your integrity.

32. Make your choices on purpose, not by default.

"You can preach a better sermon with your life than with your lips."

~ Oliver Goldsmith

33. Learn about people by listening to the questions they ask.

34. Affiliate yourself with people from a variety of occupations.

"The great men and women of the world aren't necessarily smarter than the rest, they just know the right people to ask for advice."

~ The Mastermind

35.	Take time to write down your thoughts.

36.	Silence will guide if you only listen.

"What the inner voice says will not disappoint the hoping soul."

~ Friedrich Schiller

37. When negotiating, allow the other party to make the first offer.

38. Speak with conviction and confidence.

38

"Even if you persuade me you won't persuade me."

~ Aristophanes

39. Never criticize the person; instead, focus on the behavior or action. Always be specific.

40. Treat people as humans, not transactions.

"Love communicates many wonderous things."

~ The Mastermind

41. Laugh at least twenty times a day.

42. Interject humor whenever possible, but be careful to keep it in good taste.

"Laughter is inner jogging."

~ Norman Cousins

43. Make a conscious effort to remember names.

44. Do something nice for someone without letting them know.

"You give but little when you give of your possessions. It is when you give of yourself that you truly give."

~ Kahlil Gibran

45

45. Under-promise, over-deliver.

46. Be on time, even early, to every appointment.

"You cannot display more integrity than you actually have."

~ The Mastermind

47. People have an inherent desire to perform well, so let them know your expectations and how they can achieve them.

48. Find hidden treasures by listening not to what people say, but to how they say it.

"Be hearty in your approbation
and lavish in your praise."

~ Dale Carnegie

49. Understand the dynamics of a relationship before you define expectations.

50. Communicate with individuals who have diverse backgrounds.

"If the doors of perception were cleansed everything would appear as it is...infinite."

~ William Blake

51. Take every opportunity to compliment the ideas and work of other people.

52. Build people up and you build yourself up simultaneously.

"You can't take a step up if you are busy pushing others down."

~ The Mastermind

53

53. Carefully evaluate the source before relying on advice.

54. Take time to give feedback to individuals becuase people want to know how they are doing, good or bad.

"The advice of a wise man refreshes like water from a mountain spring."

~ Proverbs

55. Identify your motives before offering advice or giving feedback.

56. Talk about the good; emphasize the positive.

"Each man sees what he carries
in his own heart."

~ Johann Wolfgang von Goethe

57.   To effectively communicate, you occasionally have to be bigger than the next person.

58.   Understand the difference between empathy and sympathy.

"Seek first to understand, then to be understood."

~ Stephen R. Covey

59. Practice silence and you will find truth.

60. Some people really enjoy hearing themselves speak, but don't be one of them.

"It is better to keep silent and let people think you are a fool than to open your mouth and remove all doubt."

~ Abraham Lincoln

61. Remember that at the end of a long stream of "no's," awaits "yes."

62. Realize there is always a solution to any challenge you may face.

"I think and think for months and years. Ninety-nine times the conclusion is always false. The hundredth time I am right."

~ Albert Einstein

63. When meeting new people, introduce yourself first.

64. Think of consequences before you answer.

"First say to yourself what you would be; and then do what you have to do."

~ Epictetus

65. Accept others for who they are not for who you want them to be.

66. Never settle for "because," as it tends to breed mediocrity.

"Unconventional thinking gets things done."

~ The Mastermind

67. When you plan a meeting, have an agenda—then follow it.

68. Don't tell people what to do— show them.

"One of the highest compliments you could ever be paid is to be told that you are a person of your word."

~ Denis Waitley

69. Children are as intelligent as you let them be.

70. When you choose to say "no," come up with alternatives.

"Children are like sponges; they absorb everything."

~ The Mastermind

71. Avoid spreading rumors or engaging in gossip.

72. When you're with someone, be proud to introduce them to others.

"If you do not tell the truth about yourself, you cannot tell it about other people."

~ Virginia Woolf

73. The way to any goal is to create a mental picture of yourself accomplishing it.

74. Write down your goals and read them often.

"You will miss everything you don't aim for."

~ The Mastermind

75. Change what is under your control and focus on the positive.

76. Relay information in a positive light; it's more likely to be absorbed.

"Nothing is good or bad, but thinking makes it so."

~ William Shakespeare

77. If you do not know how to do something—ask.

78. If you do not know how to spell a word—look it up.

"Knowledge is of two kinds: We know a subject ourselves, or we know where to find information upon it."

~ Samuel Johnson

79. Make time to talk to the ones you love.

80. When someone compliments you, say "thank you."

"Nothing in the world makes a woman more beautiful than the belief that she is beautiful."

~ Sophia Loren

81. Always speak to yourself in the positive.

82. Let your last thought of the day be a positive one.

"Self-suggestion is the creator
of character."

~ Napoleon Hill

83. Pay your bills on time. And if you can't, contact your creditor.

84. Thank all customers both in person and in writing.

"People respond more to what you do than to what you say."

~ The Mastermind

85. People are more likely to respond to you when a smile is involved.

86. Smile when you answer the phone.

"There is never a reason not to smile."

~ Peter Moon

87. Keep negative thoughts to yourself.

88. Always close conversations on a positive note; it sets the tone for your next interaction.

"Appreciate the joy of building up others."

~ The Mastermind

89. Watch how others communicate
     and determine what works and
     what does not.

90. Remember: people respond much
     better when they are asked rather
     than told.

"The superior man is modest in his speech, but exceeds in his actions."

~ Confucius

91. If you are solving a large portion of
     other people's problems, you will
     earn their respect.

92. Give credit when credit is due, and
     much of it will reflect back on you.

"The credit belongs to the person who convinces the world, not to the one to whom the idea occurs."

~ Sir F. Darwin

93. Examine all options before deciding.

94. Use open-ended questions to gain information, close-ended questions to gain agreement.

"Ask questions; discovery is the fuel of competitive advantage."

~ Jay Abraham

95. Listen to children. They have not developed filters in their thinking.

96. Children are the trailblazers of tomorrow, so teach them to pursue the path less traveled.

"Imagination is more important than knowledge."

~ Albert Einstein

97. Bring successful people into your life.

98. When you want to meet someone, simply introduce yourself.

"The common denominator of success and happiness is other people."

~ The Mastermind

99. Treat communication with care and respect—all communication is significant.

100. How you communicate with others depends on how you communicate with yourself...Keep a journal!

"How you communicate with other people will ultimately determine your success."

~ The Mastermind

101. Don't allow negative past occurrences with people determine how you treat others in the future.

102. Practice forgiveness until it becomes part of you.

"You can't shake hands with a clenched fist."

~ Indira Gandhi

103. Ask yourself, "How many people do I know that are truly good listeners, and who are they?"

104. Choose someone who is a great listener and model what they do.

"Nature has given us two ears
but only one mouth."

~ Benjamin Disraeli

105. Welcome new friends into your life.

106. Be open to making a mistake but with the possibility of succeeding as well.

"You have to accept whatever comes and the only important thing is that you meet it with the best you have to give."

~ Eleanor Roosevelt

107. Spend at least five minutes a day in prayer and meditation.

108. When meditating, imagine a large, bright yellow sun, shining down on you and evaporating negative energy.

"Hate is like acid. It can damage the vessel in which it is stored as well as destroy the object on which it is poured."

~ Ann Landers

109. Since now is all you have, resolve to forgive those who have violated you in the past.

110. Use this affirmation: "I forgive myself and others easily and honestly."

"The weak can never forgive.
Forgiveness is the attribute of
the strong."

~ Mahatma Gandhi

111. Create a list of people with whom you want to have relationships.

112. Keep this book somewhere you can see it regularly to help realign your focus.

"Whatever you steadfastly direct your attention to, will come into your life and dominate it."

~ Emmet Fox

113. Join and <u>GET INVOLVED</u> with a civic organization.

114. Organize all of your co-workers and donate money to feed and buy presents for a needy family this holiday season.

"Never doubt that a small group of thoughtful, committed citizens can change the world. Indeed, it is the only thing that ever has."

~ Margaret Mead

115. Have the courage to say, "No," when being pressured to do something you don't want to do.

116. Keep your decisions consistent with your principles.

If it ever came to a choice between compromising my principles and the performance of my duties, I know I would go with my moral principles."

~ Norman Schwarzkopf

117. Donate one hour per week to your favorite charity.

118. Be a role model for the people who are in your immediate environment.

"Do not wait for leaders; do it alone, person to person."

~ Mother Teresa

119. Be an example of desired behavior rather than telling people what to do.

120. Demonstrate confidence, enthusiasm and sincerity when communicating with other people.

"You cannot teach people anything. You can only help them discover it within themselves."

~ Galileo

121. Ask yourself this question: "What would I do if I knew I could not fail?"

122. Use this affirmation: "I act on what I know, and I am rewarded abundantly."

Ask yourself the secret of your success. Listen to your answer, and practice it."

~ Richard Bach

123. Donate twenty dollars to your local homeless shelter.

124. Help a friend or family member achieve a goal they truly want.

124

"I am only one, but still I am one.
I cannot do everything, but I can do
something. I will not refuse to do the
something I can do."

~ Helen Keller

125. Use this affirmation: "Anything is possible when I have a positive mental attitude."

126. Offer only constructive feedback when troubleshooting with others.

"Your mental attitude is your real boss."

~ Napoleon Hill

127. Send a letter of recommendation to a company who exceeded your service expectations and be sure to mention the name of the superior employee who served you.

128. When assessing performance, do it in private.

128

"When I must criticize somebody, I do it orally; when I praise somebody, I put it in writing."

~ Lee Iacocca

129. Use this phrase around children:
"You're such a good person."

130. Resolve to rid yourself of any
negative beliefs given to you by
others.

"Children are likely to live up to what you believe of them."

~ Lady Bird Johnson

131

131. Inscribe this message into your memory bank: "Assume Nothing!"

132. Give people the opportunity to make a second impression.

"People fear each other because they don't know each other. They don't know each other because they have not properly communicated with each other."

~ Martin Luther King, Jr.

133. Read a bedtime story to your child tonight.

134. Speak this phrase often: "I love you."

"We can do no great things–
only small things with great
love."

~ Mother Teresa

135. Each morning visualize the person you want to become.

136. Accept your past failures or mistakes and learn from them. Each day is a new beginning.

136

"Everyone has it within their power to say, this I am today, that I shall be tomorrow."

~ Louis L'Amour

137. Ask yourself an important question before retiring to bed at night.

138. Realize there is no such thing as a bad experience; only your interpretations can make it so.

"Learn to get in touch with silence within yourself and know that everything in this life has purpose. There are no mistakes, no coincidences, all events are blessings given to us to learn from."

~ Elizabeth Kubler-Ross

139. Instead of believing in luck, believe in yourself.

140. Plan your days in order to get the most out of the time you spend.

"I find that the harder I work,
the more luck I seem to have."

~ Thomas Jefferson

141. Identify problems as areas of improvement.

142. Always view your problems as a path to future success.

"Each problem that I solved became a rule which served afterwards to solve other problems."

~ Rene Descartes

143. Have the courage to stand up and speak out for what you believe in.

144. Friendship is communicated in many ways, so be careful what you don't say.

"In the End, we will remember
not the words of our enemies,
but the silence of our friends."

~ Martin Luther King, Jr.

145. Take the time to think. Then, equally important, take the time to do.

146. Continually think about what you want to become.

"Whether you think that you can, or that you can't, you are usually right. "

~ Henry Ford

147. If you are not able to commit to a project then do yourself a favor and don't fake it.

148. Involve yourself fully in that which you choose to do.

"The difference between 'involvement' and 'commitment' is like an eggs-and-ham breakfast; the chicken was 'involved'–the pig was 'committed'."

~ Unknown

149. Be aware of the individual realities of others.

150. Discover and know why you believe what you do.

"Reality is merely an illusion,
albeit a very persistent one. "

~ Albert Einstein

151. Remember your thoughts of childhood and the creativity they brought.

152. Avoid being a know-it-all.

"I am not young enough to know everything."

~ Oscar Wilde

153. The great thing about knowledge is that you can never have too much; keep learning.

154. Learn from everyone and every situation.

"I have never let my schooling interfere with my education."

~ Mark Twain

155. Prioritize your daily tasks in order of importance.

156. Use this affirmation: "I take action on my most important tasks first."

"Never mistake motion for action."

~ Ernest Hemingway

157. Make it a policy to never sacrifice quality.

158. Align your actions with your words.

"Well done is better than well said."

~ Benjamin Franklin

159. Learn how you learn best.

160. Attend seminars and workshops on an ongoing basis to improve your skills and talents.

"Learning is what most adults
will do for a living in the
21st century."

~ Unknown

161. Learn to communicate openly with every person with whom you come in contact.

162. Treat everyone as if they are the most important in the world... because to them they are.

"The man who goes alone can start today; but he who travels with another must wait till that other is ready."

~ Henry David Thoreau

163. Use this affirmation: "I have a positive mental attitude and contribute positive energy to the world."

164. Focus on the positive to align the energy of your life.

"A pessimist sees the difficulty in every opportunity; an optimist sees the opportunity in every difficulty."

~ Winston Churchill

165. Stop worrying about today's problems; focus on tomorrow's opportunities.

166. Average people don't take many risks—choose to be extraordinary!

"The concept is interesting and well-formed, but in order to earn better than a 'C', the idea must be feasible."

~ A Yale University management professor in response to student Fred Smith's paper proposing reliable overnight delivery service (Smith went on to found Federal Express Corp.)

167. Choose your arguments carefully, and after each one, ask yourself if there was a better way.

168. Resolve potential problems before they begin.

"The right to swing my fist
ends where the other man's
nose begins."

~ Oliver Wendell Holmes

169. Think twice before you act.

170. Ask yourself this question: "Is this going to matter in 10 years?"

"Whatever is begun in anger
ends in shame. "

~ Benjamin Franklin

171. Remember it is important not only to know what to say, but when to say it.

172. Make a minor change in thought to create a major change in outcome.

"We are not retreating—we are advancing in another direction."

~ General Douglas MacArthur

173. Help others by giving them the truth they need.

174. Be careful what you think to be true; things change quickly.

"The truth is more important
than the facts. "

~ Frank Lloyd Wright

175. Miracles happen every second of every day, so notice them.

176. If you want to believe in miracles, look into a baby's eyes.

"There are only two ways to live your life. One is as though nothing is a miracle. The other is as though everything is a miracle."

~ Albert Einstein

177. Schedule 5 appointments per year with people you admire and respect as your role models.

178. Continually ask questions and be inquisitive.

"People seldom improve when they have no other model but themselves to copy after."

~ Oliver Goldsmith

179. Praise others with genuine sincerity when they deserve it.

180. A good rule: Use positive reinforcement 4 times as much as constructive feedback.

"Praise, like gold and diamonds, owes its value to its scarcity."

~ Unknown

181. Be true to your morals and values on a consistent basis.

182. Live in humility under any and all circumstances.

"Adversity reveals genius,
prosperity conceals it."

~ Horace

183. Take the time to communicate with yourself on deeper levels.

184. Sit silently in a room with absolutely no distractions for one hour, after which you'll know why!

"The nice thing about meditation is that it makes doing nothing quite respectable."

~ Paul Dean

185. Spend more time with people who are willing to help you with your dreams.

186. Meet on a regular basis with positive-minded individuals.

"Those who agree with us may not be right but we admire their astuteness."

~ Cullen Hightower

187

187. Ask yourself what a balanced lifestyle looks like, then work toward achieving it.

188. Whenever possible, communicate face-to-face.

"What the world really needs is more love and less paperwork."

~ Pearl Bailey

189. Interrogations seldom reveal all of the information, so question with tact and respect.

190. Never walk away from a conversation with uncertainties, especially if it's with your boss or customer.

"I never learn anything talking.
I only learn things when I ask
questions."

~ Lou Holtz

191. Make the jump from looking at customers as a source of revenue to a source of inspiration to satisfy.

192. Make sure you always have "Thank You" cards, and don't be afraid to use them.

"The absolute fundamental aim
is to make money out of
satisfying customers."

~ Sir John Egan

193. Share freely with everyone, especially those who make a living from your tips.

194. Think of all the assets in your company...did you include the people?

"Wealth is something you acquire so you can share it, not keep it."

~ LaDonna Harris

195. Even a small child can read your effort...commit and deliver.

196. Communicate with a blend of passion and purpose.

"Great dancers are not great because of their technique; they are great because of their passion."

~ Martha Graham

197

197. Consistently read personal
      development books and practice
      what you learn.

198. Communicate success to yourself,
      and success will be communicated
      back.

"To be a winner, all you need to
give is all you have."

~ Unknown

Afterword

"All great achievements are the result of a multiplicity of minds working together harmoniously."

Napoleon Hill

What is the Mastermind?

The Mastermind represents one of the most powerful components of success. It's genesis can be traced to the life of the great steel magnet, Andrew Carnegie. Carnegie commissioned Napoleon Hill to produce the first philosophy of The Science of Personal Achievement. Contained within this philosophy were 17 principles of success, one of them being

the "Master Mind" principle. The principle states that when two or more minds combine their energy, experience and knowledge to a common goal, the results are infinitely multiplied. In simplest form, one plus one does not equal two, one plus one, in unison, is infinite.

Our underlying objective is to assist in the growth and development of each other and everyone that come into our lives. We hope you enjoy this collection and that it benefits your communications.

For bulk purchase of this book contact us at:
550 California Ave., Reno, Nevada 89509.
Or call: **1.800.547.9868.**

About the Authors

Jeffrey Lawrence Benjamin has for more than a decade passionately researched human achievement to fulfill his mission of sharing with his audiences valuable principles and strategies that produce immediate, positive results. By the age of 29, Jeff had already published three books to help get his message out to the world. His formal education in the field of Speech Communications is accentuated by an emphasis in corporate training. As a co-founder of BREAKTHROUGH TRAINING and performance coach helping thousands of people every year, Jeff's business specialties range from real estate and banking to management consulting and professional sales. His purposeful style is guaranteed to motivate and inspire any audience to achieve new levels of success and confidence.

John Oliver's work has taken him around the world and his diverse educational background includes degrees in English, Criminal Justice and Physical Education. John has shared that knowledge and his experiences in

the global market with several Fortune 500 companies. He is the co-founder of Breakthrough Training, a company committed to providing strategies that inspire and energize people to take immediate action toward their personal and professional transformation. John resides in Reno, Nevada with his wife and three children.

MIKE KITSON is founder and president of On-Call Graphics, Inc., a full-service advertising, graphics and printing firm. He has published 10 books and has coauthored the books <u>Quotes to Remember, A Guide to Wisdom</u> and <u>How to Get What You Want Now!, Real Life Habits for Success</u>. He is also the founder of Forward Thinking Consultants, a company specializing in one-on-one business development. Mike has a B.A. in Journalism. He has been nominated and selected for Who's Who in Executives and Professionals and is a Life Member of The National Registry of Who's Who. Mike lives in Reno, Nevada with his wife and three children.

Lloyd Barnes currently works as a marketing director in the highly competitive and evolving managed health care arena. He successfully

secured more than $10 million dollars in less than a year by using various marketing and communication principles. He comes from a human resources background with proven sales and marketing experience.

Todd Rich is a human resources professional and has used various communication principles to oversee the compensation program for large regional organization. He as a degree in Business Administration. Todd's focus is on Corporate Human Resource Management.